Wood

Many things are made of wood.

This bat is made of wood.

Paper

Many things are made
of paper.

This book is made of paper.

Here are some more things made of wood.

toy aeroplane

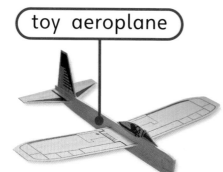

toy truck

chair

fan

Index

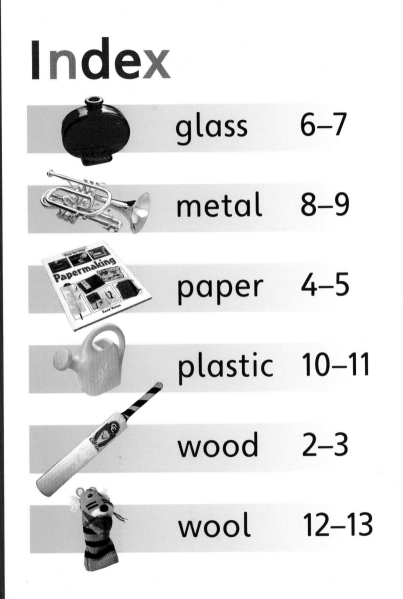

Here are some more things made of paper.

paper plate

wrapping paper

cardboard

tissues

Glass

Many things are made of glass.

These bottles are made of glass.

Here are some more things made of glass.

ornament

marbles

jars

glass

Metal

Many things are made of metal.

This trumpet is made of metal.

Here are some more things made of metal.

can

keys

fork

nails and screws

Plastic

Many things are made of plastic.

This watering can is made of plastic.

Here are some more things made of plastic.

sandals

hard hat

bucket and spade

toy truck

Wool

Many things are made of wool.

This puppet is made of wool.

Here are some more things made of wool.

knitted toys

socks

jumper

rug

Materials

Can you remember what these things are made of?